\- To my future children

Making new friends can be scary, but friends make life more fun!

THE DOODLES AND THE POODLE

By: Kaylee Benge

There once were two Doodles who were the best of friends.

hey did everything together and that is the way it had been
orever.

One day, the Doodles were playing tug of war when the owners came walking in through the front door.

4

heir owners brought home something strange and the oodles realized that their lives were about to change.

The Doodles had fear in their eyes and did not know what to do with the new surprise.

As their owners placed the surprise on the floor, a Poodle ran towards them all the way from the door.

The Doodles continued to play and ignored the Poodle every way.

When the Poodle realized they were not paying him any mind,
e went to the corner and started to whine.

The Poodle thought, "What did I do wrong? Why do I no
belong?"

As the Doodles continued to play, they saw the poodle
...eary-eyed...where he lay.

One of the Doodles saw the poodle where he lay all sad an
had an idea that was not half bad.

he Doodle ran over to the Poodle and said, "come and join us
ow" and gave him a friendly, playful bow.

The Poodle hopped up and ran over from where he lay, grabbe the rope and started to play.

fter all the playing was said and done, they all agreed that wo friends are better than one.

Meet the Doodles and the Poodle

IZZY, GRIFFEY, PIPER

IZZY

Meet Izzy. She is the oldest and the lightest color of the three. She always has a sock or a toy with her and she loves to play.

PIPER

Meet Piper Doodle. Piper was adopted when she was 6 months old and is from the same litter as Izzy. She loves treats and snacks.

GRIFFEY

Meet GRIFFEY the Poodle. He loves to bother his sisters. Izzy and Piper took some time to warm up to him, but now the three are inseparable.

Questions after the story:

1. Why do you think the Doodles ignored the Poodle when the owners brought him home?

2. How did the Poodle feel knowing that the Doodles did not want to be friends at first?

3. How did the Poodle feel after the Doodle ask him to play?

Coloring Page to follow →

ISBN 9798729955053